United States of America

S0-BXW-172

Facts Of the 50 states in the United States, 48 are grouped together on the land between Canada and Mexico.

 Paste the sticker to complete the map. After pasting, point out and say "United States of America."

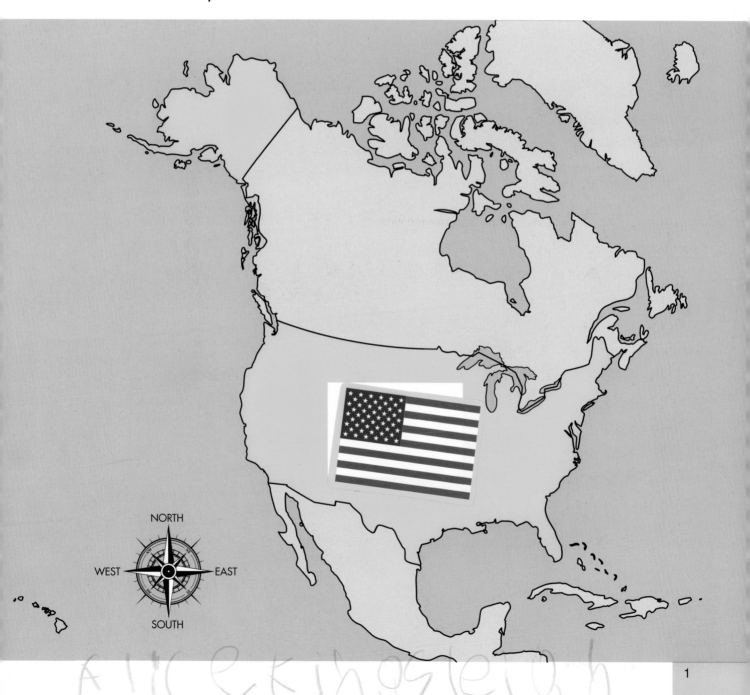

Five Regions

Facts In this book, the 50 states are grouped into five regions: Northeast, Midwest, Southeast, Southwest, and West. Note that Alaska is scaled down in the map below.

 Paste the stickers to complete the map. After pasting, point out and say "Northeast," "Midwest," "Southeast," "Southwest," and "West."

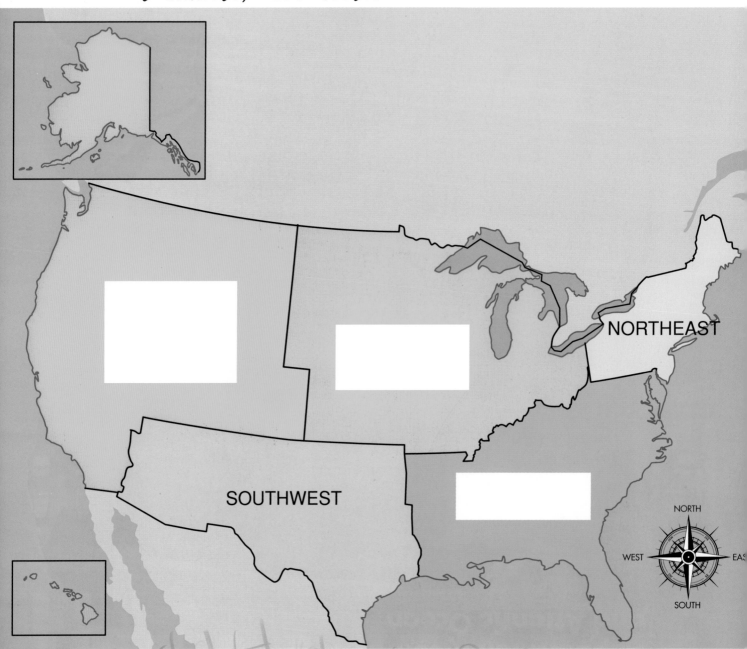

NORTHEAST

SOUTHWEST

NORTH

WEST   EAS

SOUTH

Chapter 1
The Northeast
Maine and Vermont

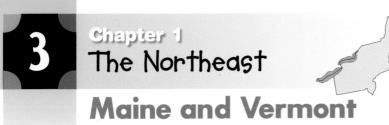

Facts Maine is bordered by Canada to the north. Vermont is also bordered by Canada to the north. Note that each region map in this book is based on the map on page 2.

 Paste the stickers to complete the map. After pasting, point out and say "Maine" and "Vermont."

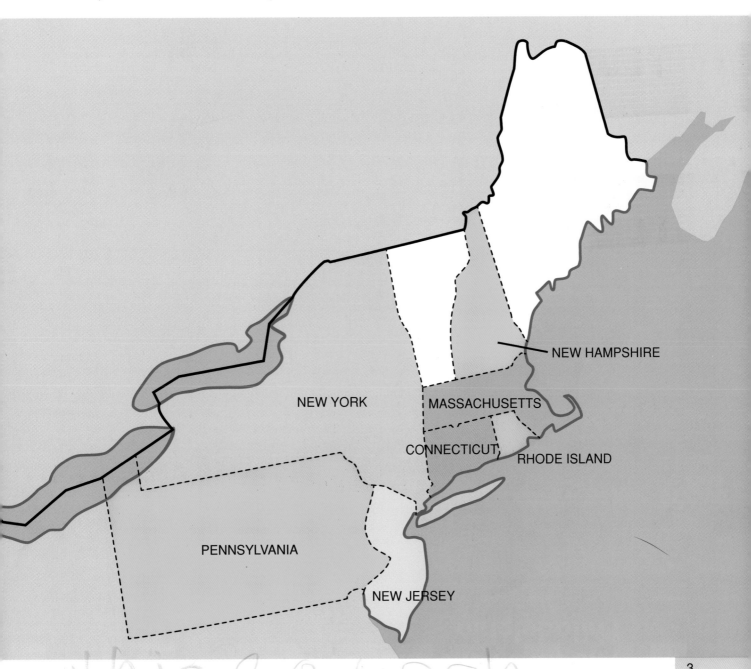

NEW HAMPSHIRE

NEW YORK

MASSACHUSETTS

CONNECTICUT

RHODE ISLAND

PENNSYLVANIA

NEW JERSEY

Chapter 1
The Northeast

New Hampshire, New Jersey, and Rhode Island

Facts New Hampshire is bordered by Canada to the north. Newark is the biggest city in New Jersey. Rhode Island is the smallest state in the United States.

 Paste the stickers to complete the map. After pasting, point out and say "New Hampshire," "New Jersey," and "Rhode Island."

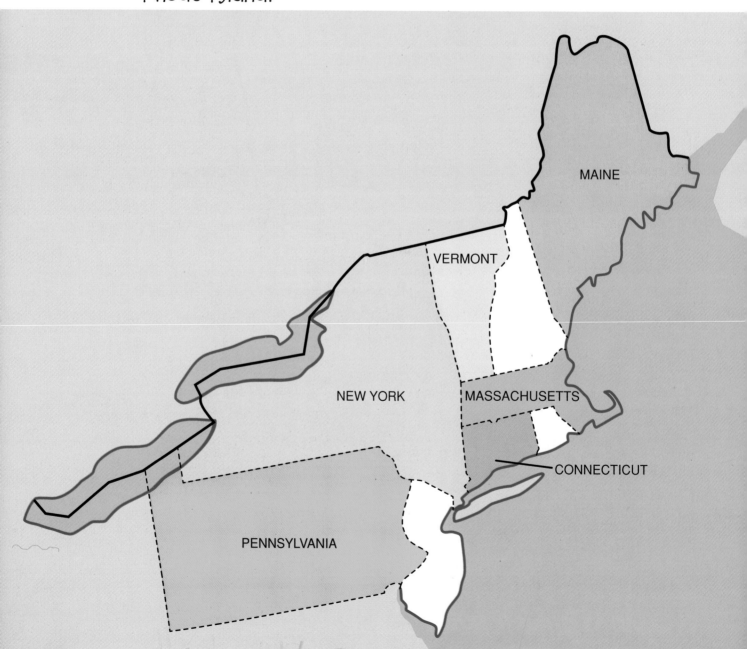

MAINE

VERMONT

NEW YORK   MASSACHUSETTS

CONNECTICUT

PENNSYLVANIA

Chapter 1
The Northeast

Boston and New York City

Facts Boston is Massachusetts's state capital and its biggest city. New York City is the biggest city in the United States.

Paste the stickers to complete the map. After pasting, point out and say "Boston" and "New York City."

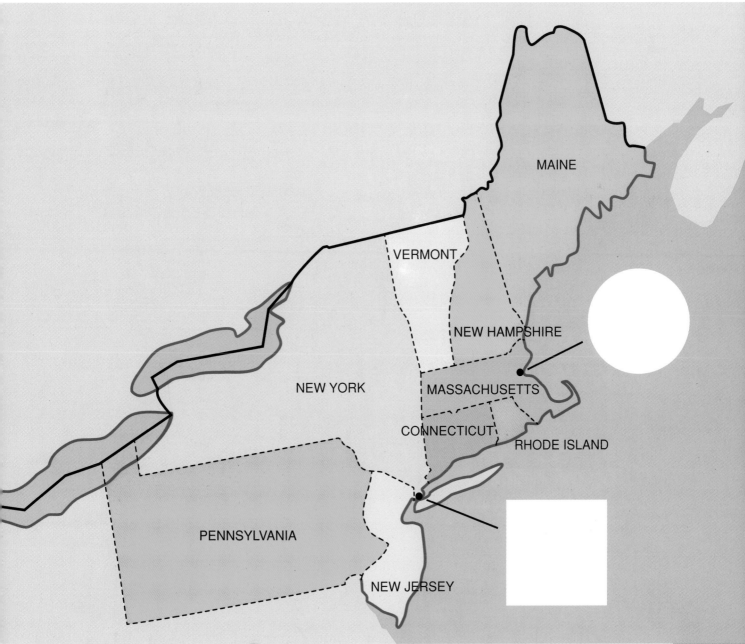

MAINE

VERMONT

NEW HAMPSHIRE

NEW YORK

MASSACHUSETTS

CONNECTICUT

RHODE ISLAND

PENNSYLVANIA

NEW JERSEY

6

Niagara Falls and Philadelphia

| **Facts** | Niagara Falls is made up of three waterfalls on the border between the United States and Canada. Philadelphia played an important role in the American Revolution. |

 Paste the stickers to complete the map. After pasting, point out and say "Niagara Falls" and "Philadelphia."

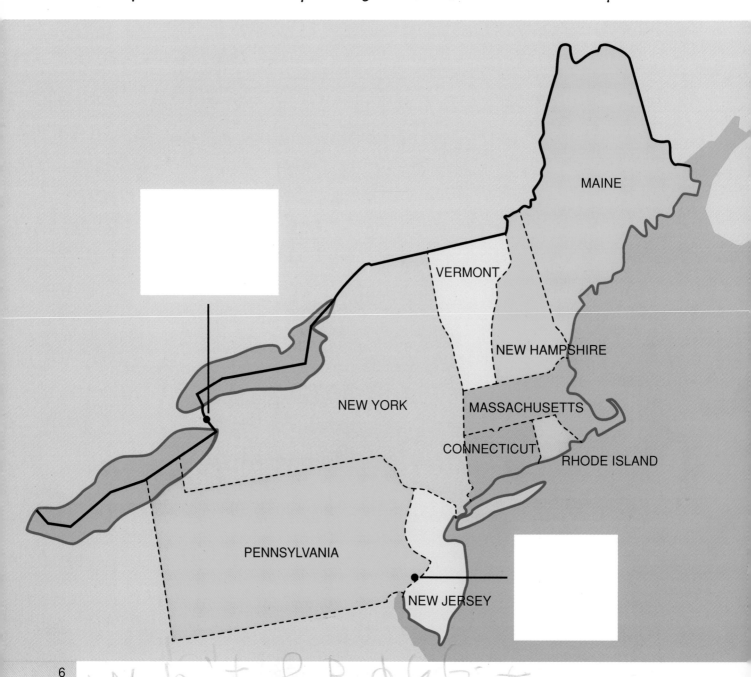

MAINE

VERMONT

NEW HAMPSHIRE

NEW YORK

MASSACHUSETTS

CONNECTICUT

RHODE ISLAND

PENNSYLVANIA

NEW JERSEY

Appalachian Mountains and Atlantic Ocean

Facts The Appalachian Mountains stretch from Newfoundland Island in Canada to Alabama. This mountain range is 1,500 miles (2,400 kilometers) long. The Atlantic Ocean borders the United States to the east.

Color the white areas. After coloring, point out and say "Appalachian Mountains" and "Atlantic Ocean."

Brown   Blue

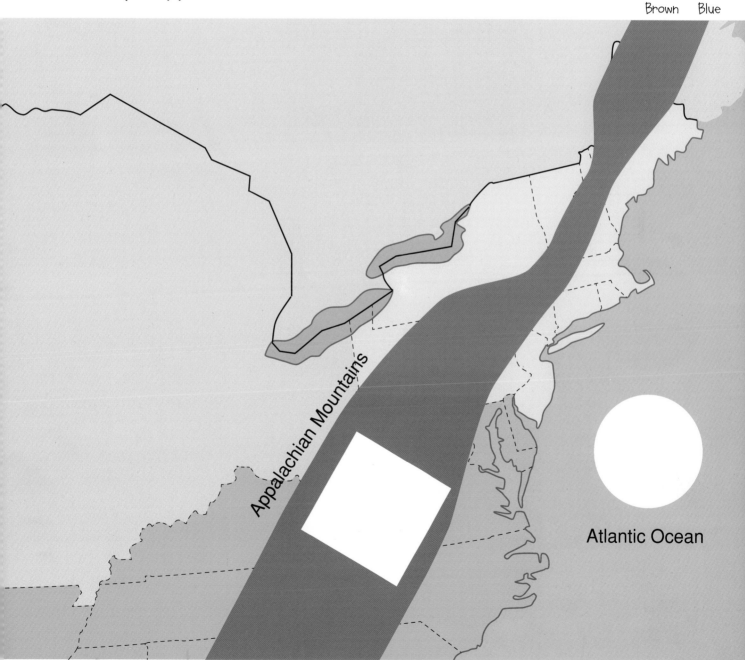

Appalachian Mountains

Atlantic Ocean

The Northeast

Plymouth Rock

MASSACHUSETTS

Plymouth Rock

Facts Some people say Plymouth Rock is the first thing the Pilgrims stepped on when they arrived in America.

Color the white areas. After coloring, point out and say "Plymouth Rock."

Pencil Blue

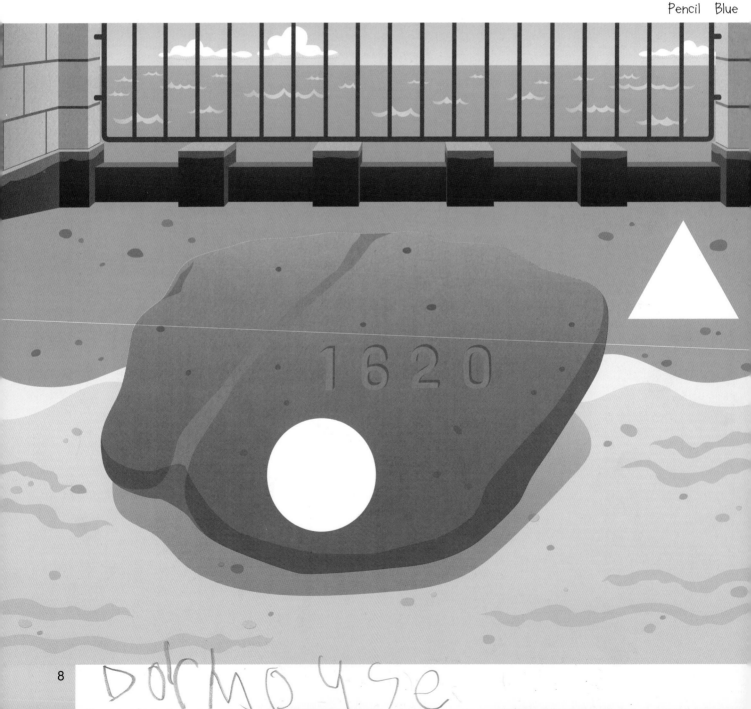

1620

DOrMOYSe

Statue of Liberty

NEW YORK

New York City

Facts — The Statue of Liberty is a sculpture on Liberty Island in New York Harbor. It was a gift from the French people.

 Draw a line through the maze from the arrow (➡) to the star (★). After finishing, say "Statue of Liberty."

The Northeast

Mystic Seaport

CONNECTICUT
Mystic Seaport

Facts   Mystic is famous for its historic seaport.

 Draw a line through the maze from the arrow (➡) to the star (★). After finishing, say "Mystic Seaport."

Chapter 2
The Midwest

Iowa and North Dakota

Facts Iowa is bordered by the Mississippi River (see page 23) on the east. Most of North Dakota is in the Great Plains (see page 15).

 Paste the stickers to complete the map. After pasting, point out and say "Iowa" and "North Dakota."

NEW HAMPSHIRE

VERMONT

MAINE

MASSACHUSETTS

MINNESOTA

SOUTH DAKOTA

WISCONSIN

NEW YORK

MICHIGAN

RHODE ISLAND

NEBRASKA

PENNSYLVANIA

CONNECTICUT

OHIO

NEW JERSEY

ILLINOIS   INDIANA

KANSAS   MISSOURI

Atlantic Ocean

The Midwest

Kansas, Ohio, and Wisconsin

Facts

Kansas is in the Great Plains (see page 15). Ohio includes part of Lake Erie, one of the Great Lakes (see page 15). Wisconsin includes parts of Lake Michigan and Lake Superior (see page 15).

Paste the stickers to complete the map. After pasting, point out and say "Kansas," "Ohio," and "Wisconsin."

NORTH DAKOTA   MINNESOTA

NEW HAMPSHIRE

VERMONT

MASSACHUSETTS

MAINE

SOUTH DAKOTA

MICHIGAN

NEW YORK

NEBRASKA

IOWA

PENNSYLVANIA

RHODE ISLA

ILLINOIS   INDIANA

CONNECTICU

NEW JERSEY

MISSOURI

Atlantic Oce

The Midwest

Chicago and Detroit

Facts Chicago is the third biggest city in the United States. Detroit is famous for the large car companies that have been based there.

 Paste the stickers to complete the map. After pasting, point out and say "Chicago" and "Detroit."

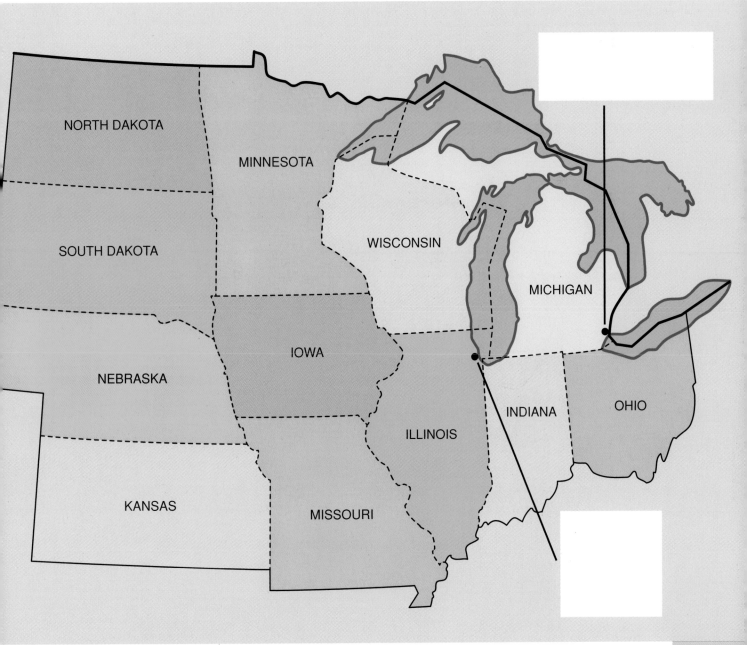

NORTH DAKOTA

MINNESOTA

SOUTH DAKOTA

WISCONSIN

MICHIGAN

IOWA

NEBRASKA

INDIANA

OHIO

ILLINOIS

KANSAS

MISSOURI

Minneapolis and St. Louis

Facts Minneapolis is north of where the Minnesota River meets the Mississippi River. St. Louis is south of where the Missouri River meets the Mississippi River (see page 23).

Paste the stickers to complete the map. After pasting, point out and say "Minneapolis" and "St. Louis."

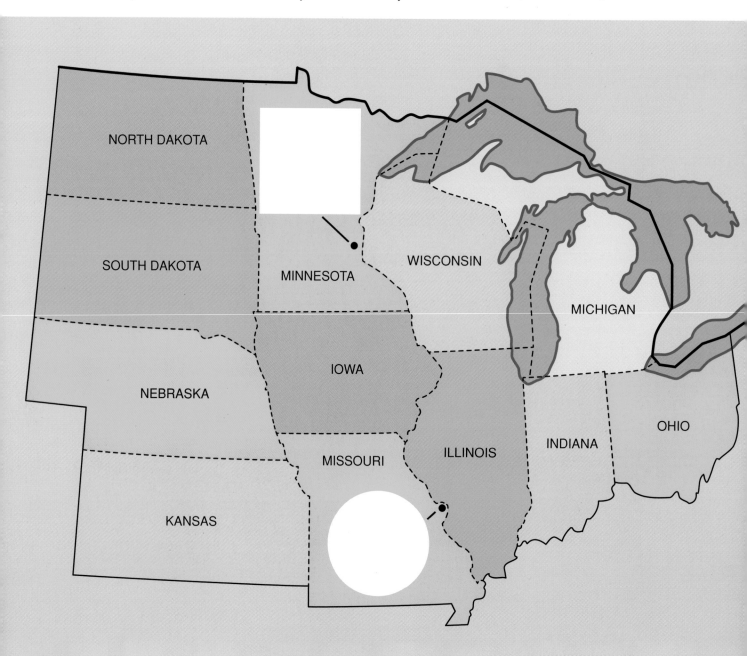

Chapter 2

The Midwest

Great Lakes and Great Plains

Facts There are five Great Lakes. Four of the five are on the border between the United States and Canada. The Great Plains is a broad range of flat land. It covers from east of the Rocky Mountains (see page 33) to most parts of North Dakota, South Dakota, Nebraska, and Kansas.

Color the white areas. After coloring, point out and say "Great Lakes" and "Great Plains."

Blue   Green

Lake Superior

Lake Huron

Lake Ontario

Great Plains

Lake Erie

Lake Michigan

Appalachian Mountains

Atlantic Ocean

Chapter 2
The Midwest

Chimney Rock

NEBRASKA

Chimney Rock

| Facts | Chimney Rock is 4,226 feet (1,288 meters) tall. In the middle of the 19th century, it was a landmark along major trails such as the Oregon Trail and the California Trail. |

Color the white area. After coloring, point out and say "Chimney Rock."

Orange

Indianapolis 500

Facts The Indianapolis 500 is a car race held annually in a suburb of Indianapolis. It is also called the Indy 500.

 Draw a line through the maze from the arrow (➡) to the star (★). After finishing, say "Indianapolis 500."

Mount Rushmore

SOUTH DAKOTA

Mount Rushmore

Facts Mount Rushmore National Memorial is a sculpture carved into the face of Mount Rushmore. It shows the heads of four United States presidents. From left, they are George Washington, Thomas Jefferson, Theodore Roosevelt, and Abraham Lincoln.

Draw a line through the maze from the arrow (➡) to the star (★). After finishing, say "Mount Rushmore."

Alabama, Arkansas, South Carolina, and Virginia

Alabama is bordered by the Gulf of Mexico to the south. You say the state name Arkansas like this: Ar-kan-saw. South Carolina is bordered by the Atlantic Ocean to the east. Virginia is bordered by the Chesapeake Bay and the Atlantic Ocean to the east.

Paste the stickers to complete the map. After pasting, point out and say "Alabama," "Arkansas," "South Carolina," and "Virginia."

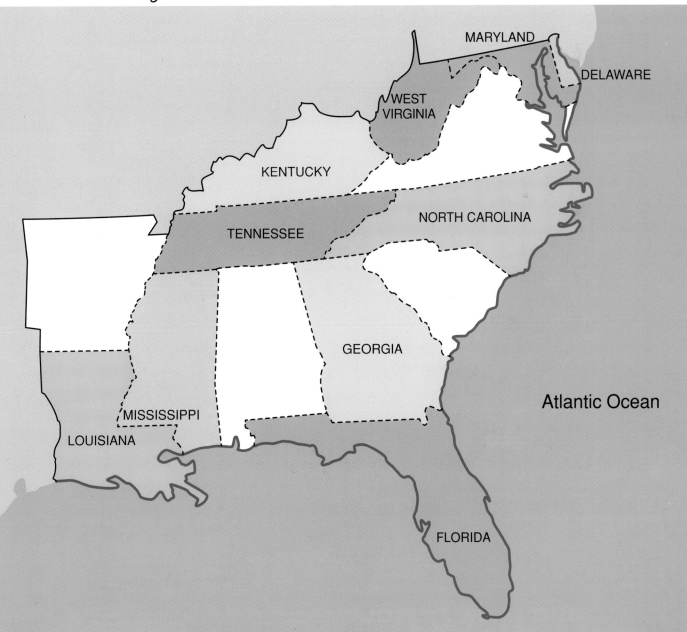

Chapter 3
The Southeast

Kentucky, Maryland, Mississippi, and North Carolina

Facts Most of eastern Kentucky is part of the Appalachian Mountains. Maryland and North Carolina are bordered by the Atlantic Ocean to the east. Mississippi is bordered by the Mississippi River (see page 23) to the west.

Paste the stickers to complete the map. After pasting, point out and say "Kentucky," "Maryland," "Mississippi," and "North Carolina."

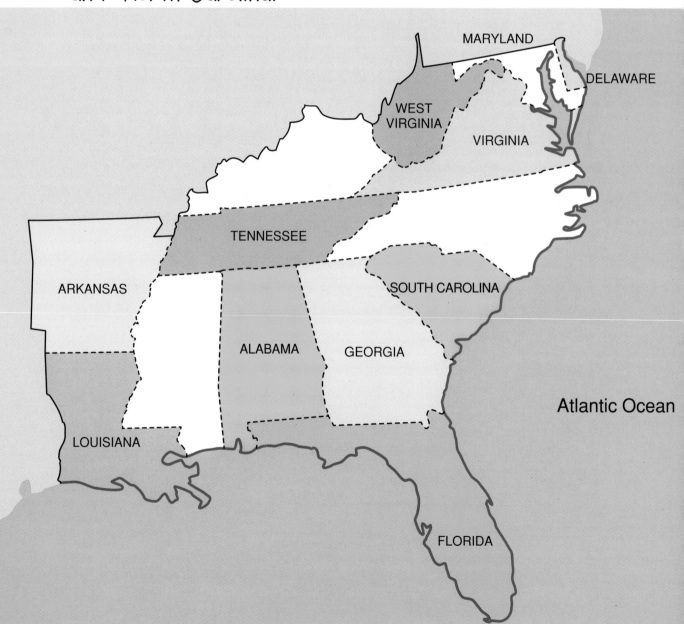

Delaware, Georgia, Tennessee, and West Virginia

Facts Delaware is the second smallest state. Atlanta is the biggest city in Georgia. Tennessee is bordered by eight states. West Virginia is located in the Appalachian Mountains.

Paste the stickers to complete the map. After pasting, point out and say "Delaware," "Georgia," "Tennessee," and "West Virginia."

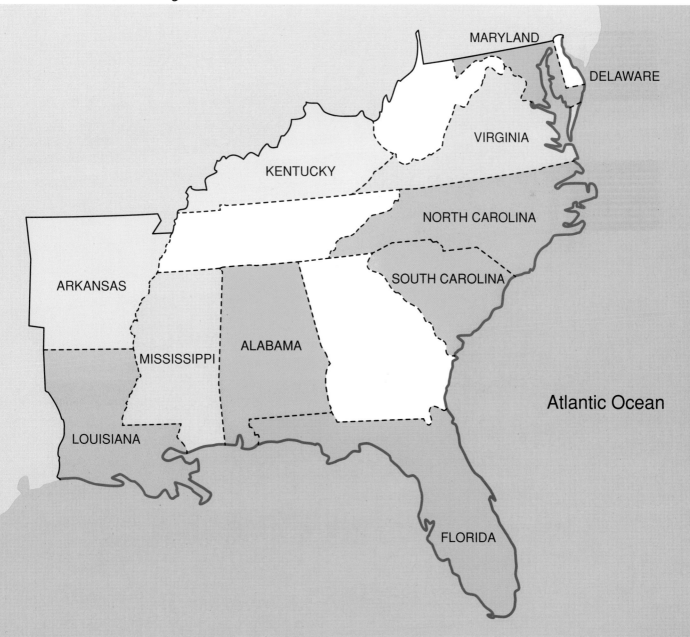

MARYLAND

DELAWARE

VIRGINIA

KENTUCKY

NORTH CAROLINA

ARKANSAS

SOUTH CAROLINA

ALABAMA

MISSISSIPPI

Atlantic Ocean

LOUISIANA

FLORIDA

Chapter 3
The Southeast
Washington, D.C., and New Orleans

Facts Washington, D.C., is the capital of the United States. It is not part of any state. It is a federal district. New Orleans is located at the mouth of the Mississippi River (see page 23).

 Paste the stickers to complete the map. After pasting, point out and say "Washington, D.C." and "New Orleans."

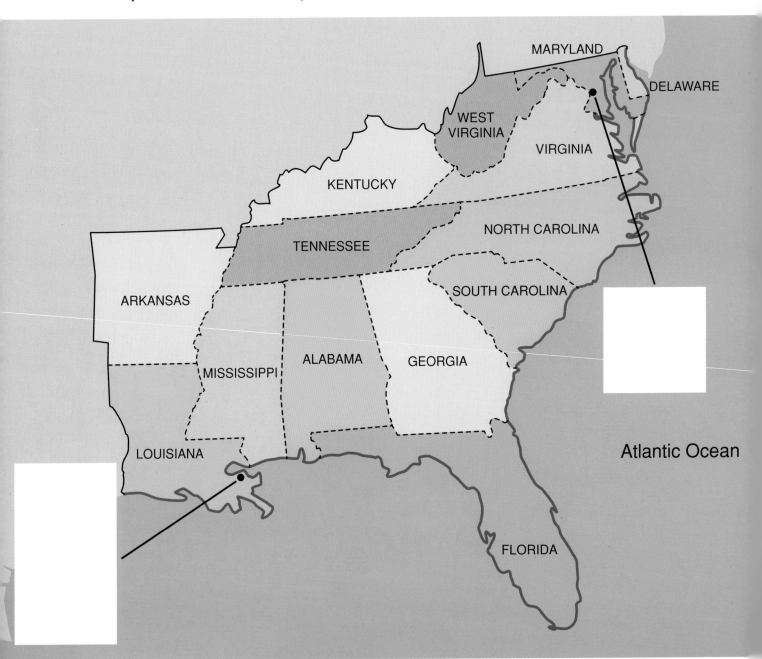

Gulf of Mexico and Mississippi River

Facts The Gulf of Mexico is bounded by the United States, Mexico, and Cuba. The Mississippi River is the longest river in the United States. It starts in Minnesota and goes to the Gulf of Mexico.

 Color the white area and trace the Mississippi River. After finishing, point out and say "Gulf of Mexico" and "Mississippi River."

Blue

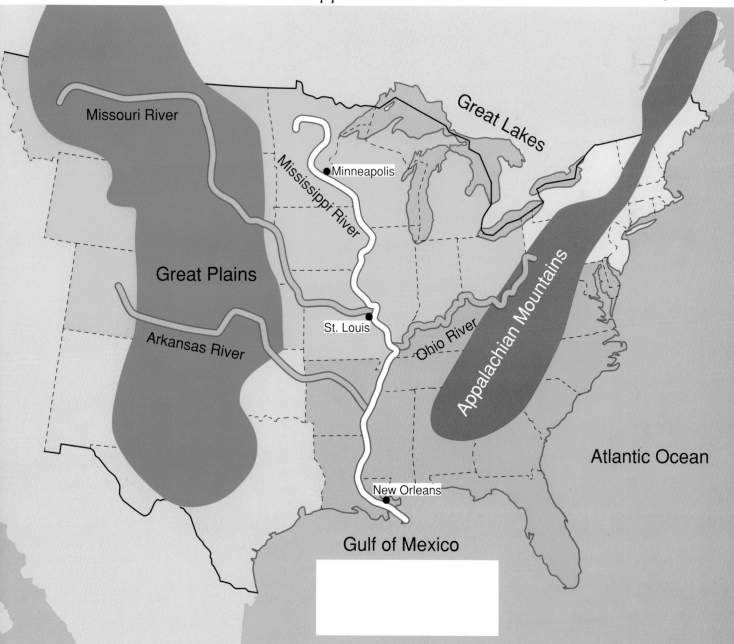

Missouri River

Great Lakes

Mississippi River

● Minneapolis

Great Plains

Arkansas River

St. Louis

Ohio River

Appalachian Mountains

Atlantic Ocean

New Orleans

Gulf of Mexico

John F. Kennedy Space Center

FLORIDA

John F. Kennedy Space Center

Facts Many spacecrafts have been launched from the John F. Kennedy Space Center. U.S. space shuttles were launched from this center.

 Draw a line through the maze from the arrow (➡) to the star (★). After finishing, say "John F. Kennedy Space Center."

Lincoln Memorial

Washington, D.C.

Facts The Lincoln Memorial was built in 1922 to honor President Abraham Lincoln.

 Draw a line through the maze from the arrow (➡) to the star (★). After finishing, say "Lincoln Memorial."

Chapter 4

The Southwest

New Mexico and Oklahoma

Facts New Mexico is bordered by Texas and Mexico to the south. In Oklahoma, more than 25 Native American languages are spoken.

Paste the stickers to complete the map. After pasting, point out and say "New Mexico" and "Oklahoma."

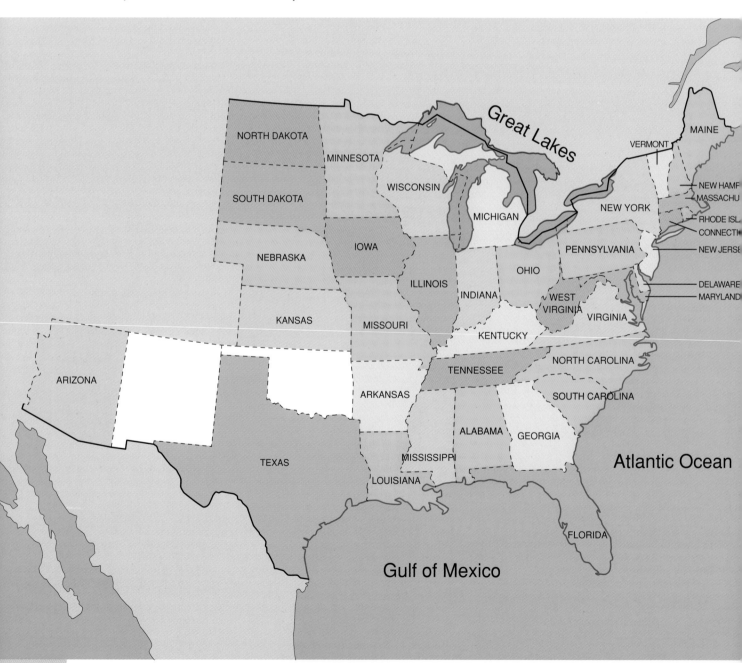

27 **Chapter 4**
The Southwest

Dallas and Houston

Facts Dallas plays an important role in the economy of the United States. Houston is the fourth biggest city in the United States.

Paste the stickers to complete the map. After pasting, point out and say "Dallas" and "Houston."

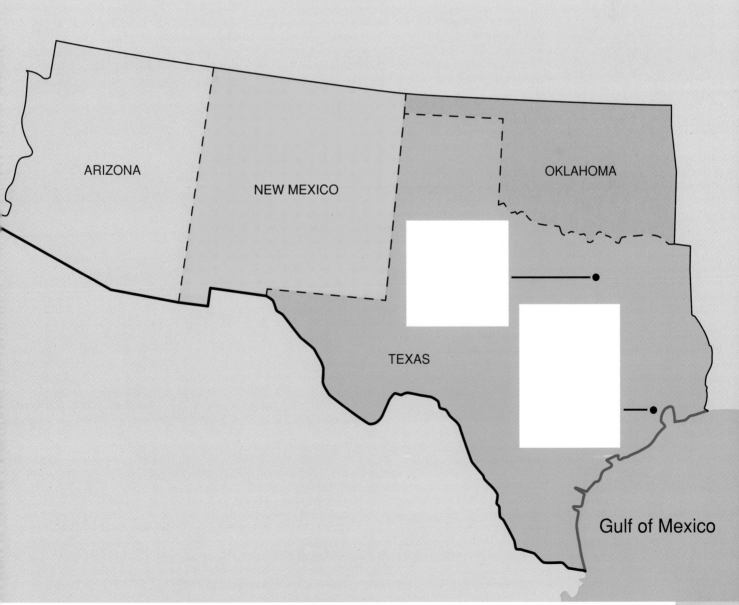

ARIZONA

NEW MEXICO

OKLAHOMA

TEXAS

Gulf of Mexico

Grand Canyon

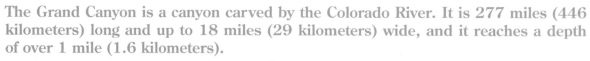

Facts

The Grand Canyon is a canyon carved by the Colorado River. It is 277 miles (446 kilometers) long and up to 18 miles (29 kilometers) wide, and it reaches a depth of over 1 mile (1.6 kilometers).

Color the white areas. After coloring, say "Grand Canyon."

Brown

The West

Alaska and Hawaii

Facts Alaska is the largest state in the United States. Hawaii is the most recent state to join the United States, and the only state composed entirely of islands.

 Paste the stickers to complete the map. After pasting, point out and say "Alaska" and "Hawaii."

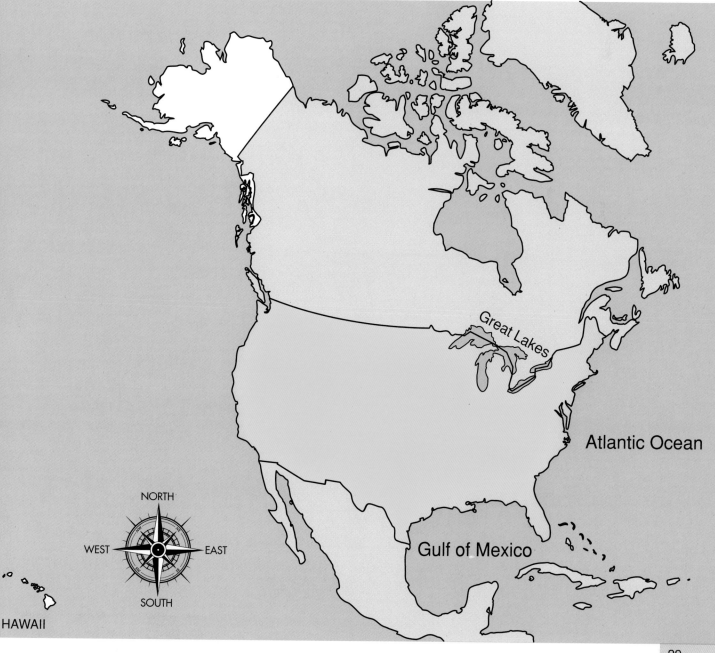

Great Lakes

Atlantic Ocean

Gulf of Mexico

NORTH

WEST — EAST

SOUTH

HAWAII

Chapter 5

The West

Colorado and Oregon

Facts	Many of the tallest peaks in the Rocky Mountains (see page 33) are in Colorado. Oregon is bordered on the west by the Pacific Ocean.

Paste the stickers to complete the map. After pasting, point out and say "Colorado" and "Oregon."

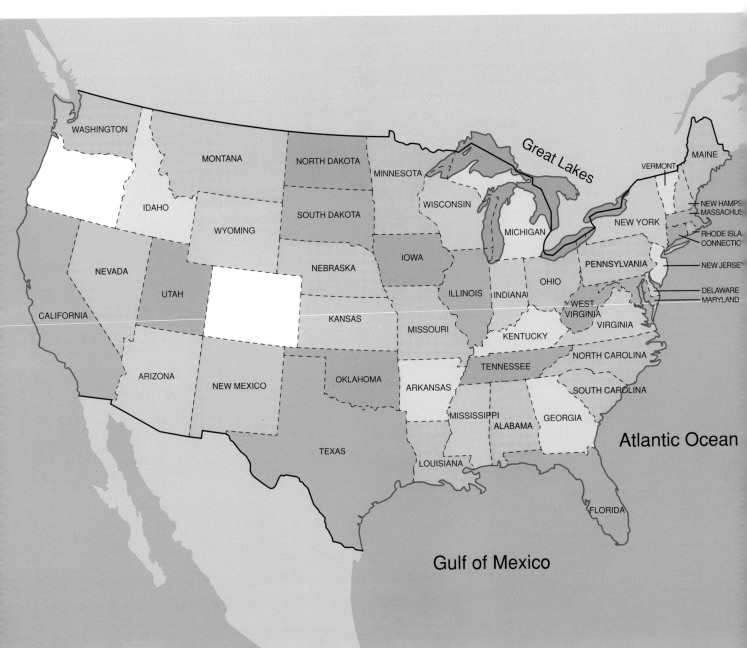

The West

Los Angeles and San Francisco

Facts Los Angeles is the second biggest city in the United States. San Francisco is widely known for its many hills.

Paste the stickers to complete the map. After pasting, point out and say "Los Angeles" and "San Francisco."

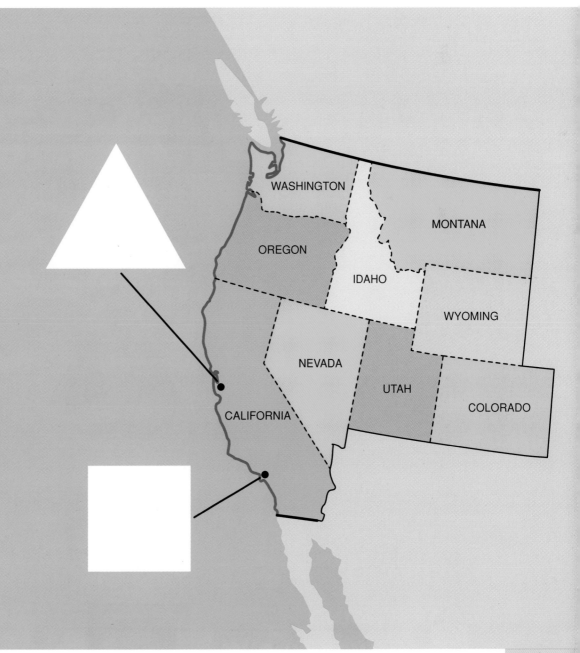

The West

Honolulu and Seattle

Facts Honolulu is Hawaii's capital and biggest city. Seattle is a seaport city and the biggest city in Washington.

 Paste the stickers to complete the map. After pasting, point out and say "Honolulu" and "Seattle."

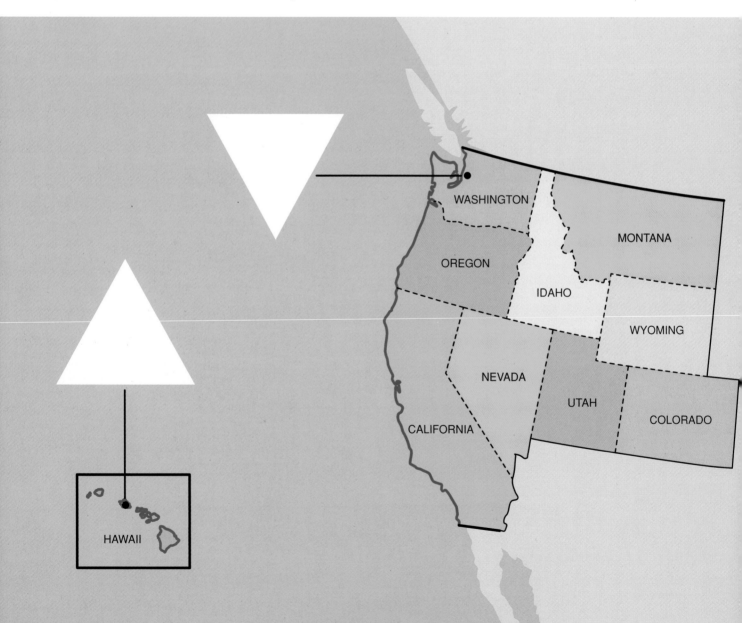

WASHINGTON

MONTANA

OREGON

IDAHO

WYOMING

NEVADA

UTAH

COLORADO

CALIFORNIA

HAWAII

Chapter 5
The West

Pacific Ocean and Rocky Mountains

Facts The Pacific Ocean is the largest ocean on Earth. The Rocky Mountains are a major mountain range in western North America. They stretch more than 3,000 miles (4,800 kilometers) from Canada to New Mexico.

Color the white areas. After coloring, point out and say "Pacific Ocean" and "Rocky Mountains."

Blue   Brown

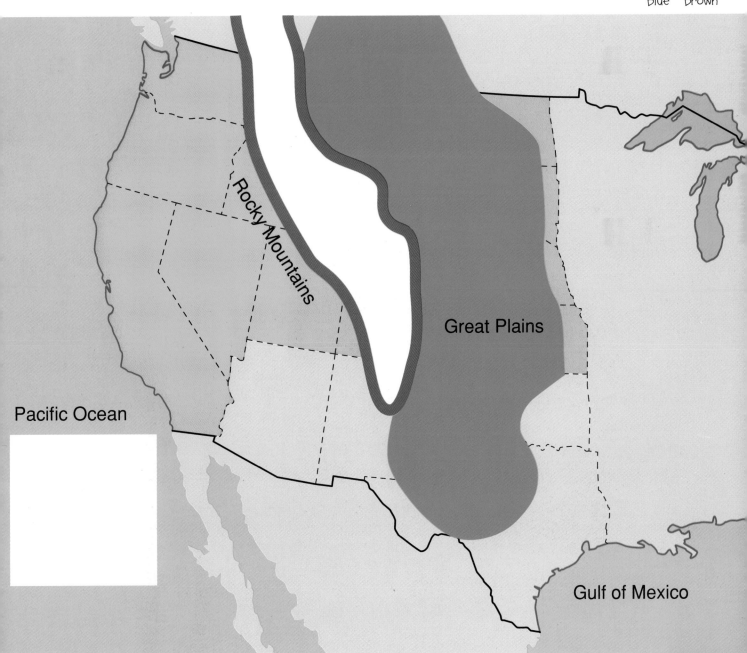

Rocky Mountains

Great Plains

Pacific Ocean

Gulf of Mexico

Yellowstone National Park

MONTANA

IDAHO

WYOMING

Yellowstone National Park

Facts Yellowstone is the first national park in the United States. It is mostly located in Wyoming, but also in Montana and Idaho.

Color the white areas. After coloring, say "Yellowstone National Park."

Brown   Black

Chapter 5
The West

Hoover Dam

NEVADA

Hoover Dam

ALIZONA

Hoover Dam is in the Black Canyon of the Colorado River, along the border between Nevada and Arizona.

 Draw a line through the maze from the arrow (➡) to the star (★). After finishing, say "Hoover Dam."

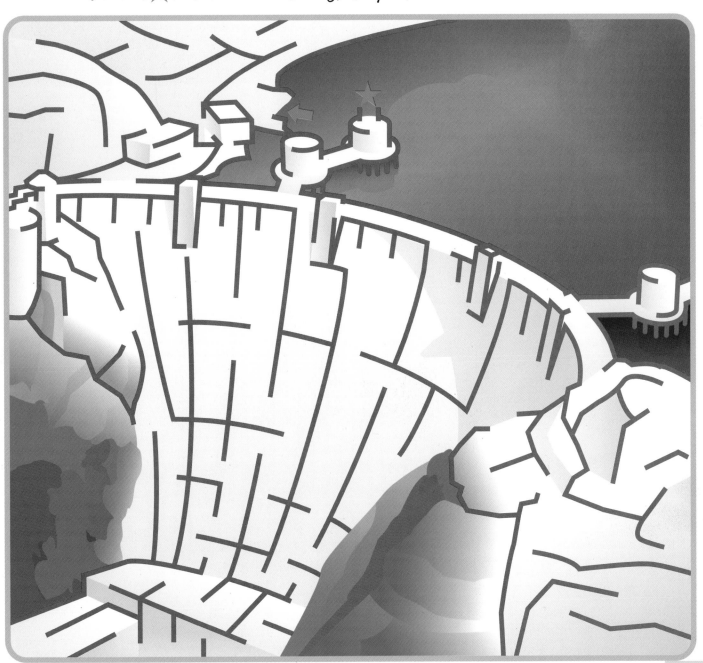

Monument Valley

UTAH

ALIZONA

Monument Valley

Facts

Monument Valley is an area along the border of Arizona and Utah. It is also close to the Four Corners area where four states meet. The four states are Colorado, New Mexico, Arizona, and Utah.

Draw a line through the maze from the arrow (➡) to the star (★). After finishing, say "Monument Valley."

Introduction
Canada

Canada

Facts Canada has ten provinces and three territories. Its border with the United States is the world's longest land border.

Paste the sticker to complete the map. After pasting, point out and say "Canada."

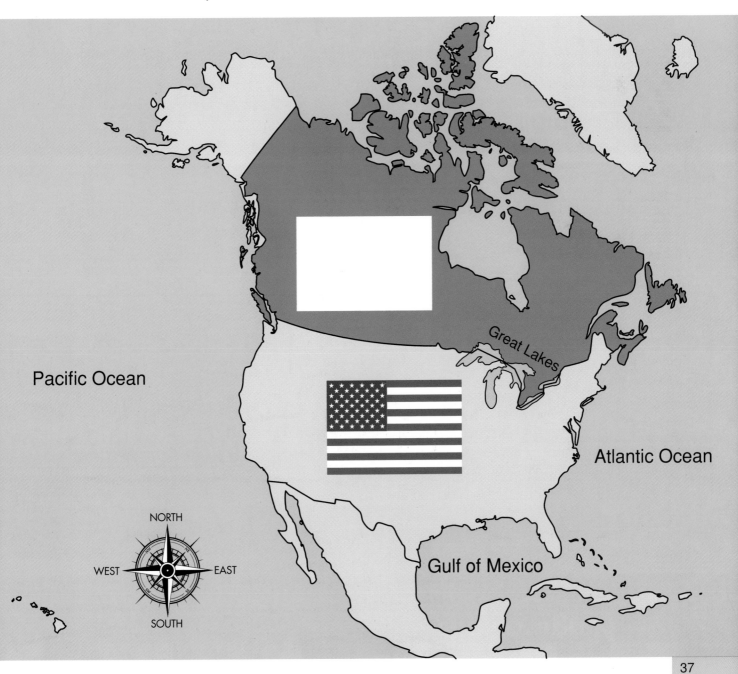

Pacific Ocean

Great Lakes

Atlantic Ocean

NORTH

WEST — EAST

Gulf of Mexico

SOUTH

New Brunswick, Newfoundland and Labrador, and Nova Scotia

Facts

New Brunswick is the only province in which English and French are official languages. Newfoundland and Labrador is the easternmost province in Canada. Nova Scotia is the second smallest province.

Paste the stickers to complete the map. After pasting, point out and say "New Brunswick," "Newfoundland and Labrador," and "Nova Scotia."

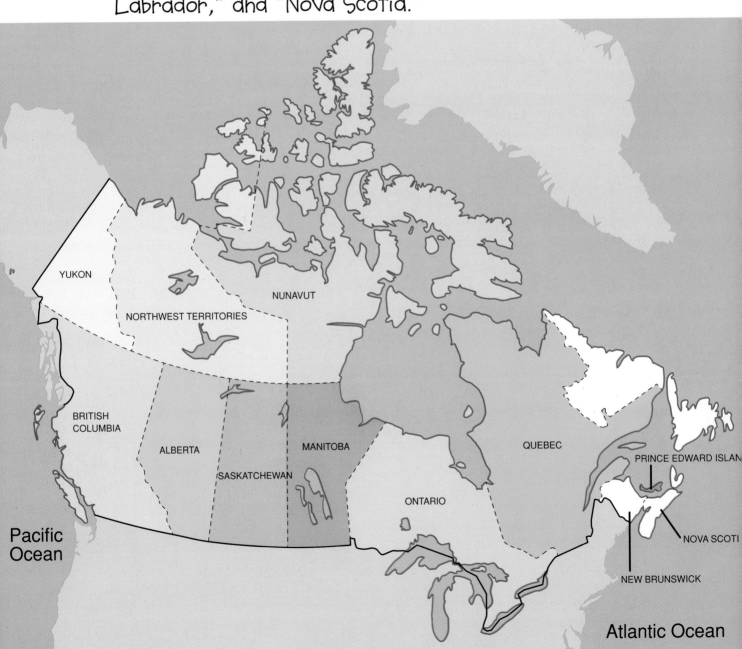

Chapter 6
Canada

Ottawa, Montreal, and Toronto

Facts Ottawa is the capital city of Canada. Montreal is the second biggest city in Canada. Toronto is the biggest city in Canada.

 Paste the stickers to complete the map. After pasting, point out and say "Ottawa," "Montreal," and "Toronto."

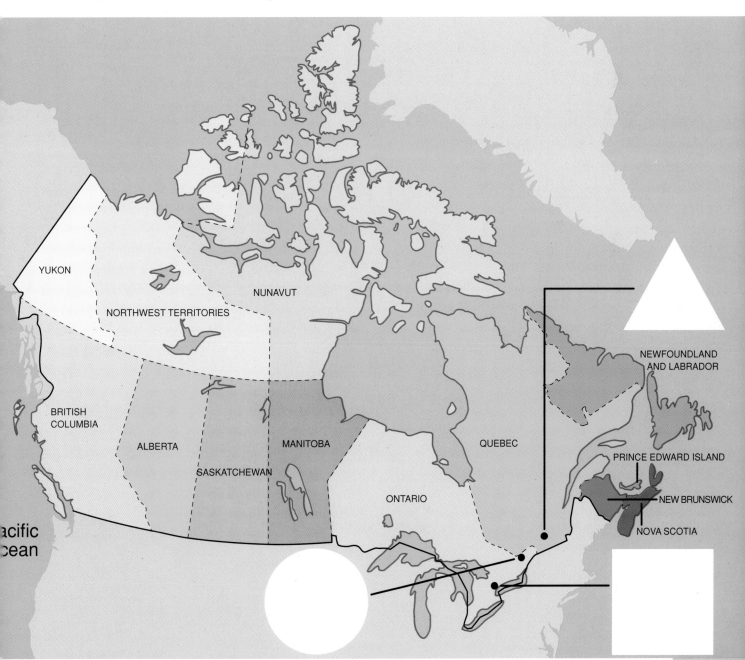

Green Gables and Niagara Falls

Facts Green Gables is a farm on Prince Edward Island. It is the setting for the Anne of Green Gables novels by Lucy Maud Montgomery. Niagara Falls is on the border of Ontario Province and New York State.

Paste the stickers to complete the map. After pasting, point out and say "Green Gables" and "Niagara Falls."

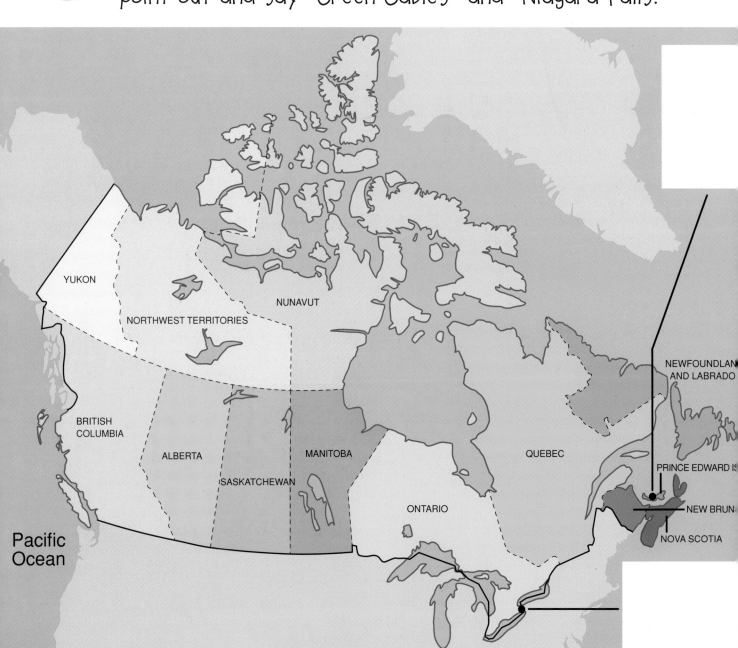

YUKON

NORTHWEST TERRITORIES

NUNAVUT

NEWFOUNDLAN AND LABRADO

BRITISH COLUMBIA

ALBERTA

MANITOBA

SASKATCHEWAN

QUEBEC

PRINCE EDWARD IS

ONTARIO

NEW BRUN

Pacific Ocean

NOVA SCOTIA

Chateau Frontenac

Facts Chateau Frontenac is located in Quebec City. Quebec City is the capital of Quebec Province. Quebec Province's official language is French.

Draw a line through the maze from the arrow (➡) to the star (★). After finishing, say "Chateau Frontenac."

Chapter 6
Canada

Northern Lights

NORTHWEST
TERRITORIES

YUKON

Dawson City Yellowknife NUNAVUT

Facts The northern lights are a natural light display in the sky. Two well-known places to see them are Yellowknife, Northwest Territories, and Dawson City, Yukon Territory.

Color the white areas. After coloring, point out and say "northern lights."

Green

Canadian Rockies and Hudson Bay

Facts The Canadian Rockies cover from the border of Yukon Territory and British Columbia Province to Alberta Province. They continue into the United States as the Rocky Mountains. All islands in the Hudson Bay belong to Nunavut Territory.

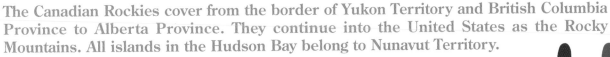

Color the white areas. After coloring, point out and say "Canadian Rockies" and "Hudson Bay."

Brown   Blue

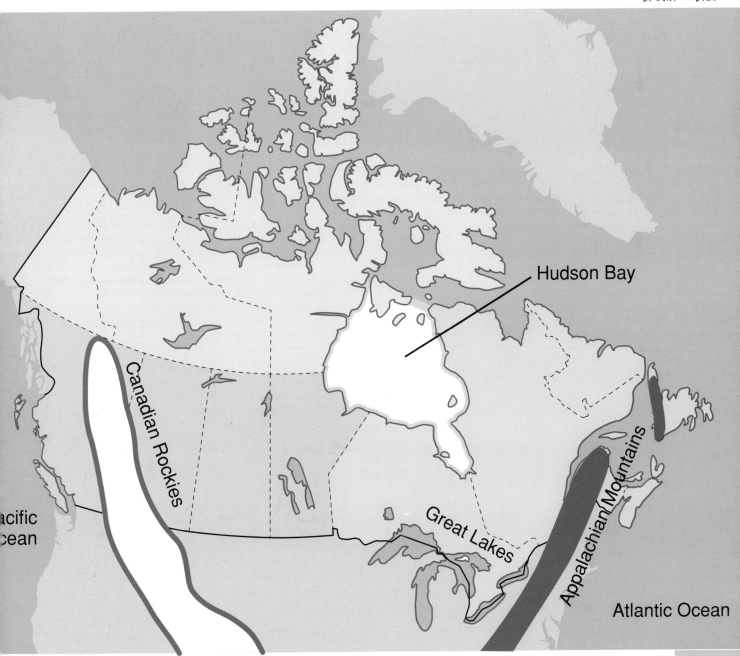

Hudson Bay

Canadian Rockies

Pacific Ocean

Great Lakes

Appalachian Mountains

Atlantic Ocean

Chapter 6
Canada

Manitoba and Saskatchewan

Facts | Manitoba Province is bordered by North Dakota and Minnesota to the south. Saskatchewan Province is bordered by North Dakota and Montana to the south.

 Paste the stickers to complete the map. After pasting, point out and say "Manitoba" and "Saskatchewan."

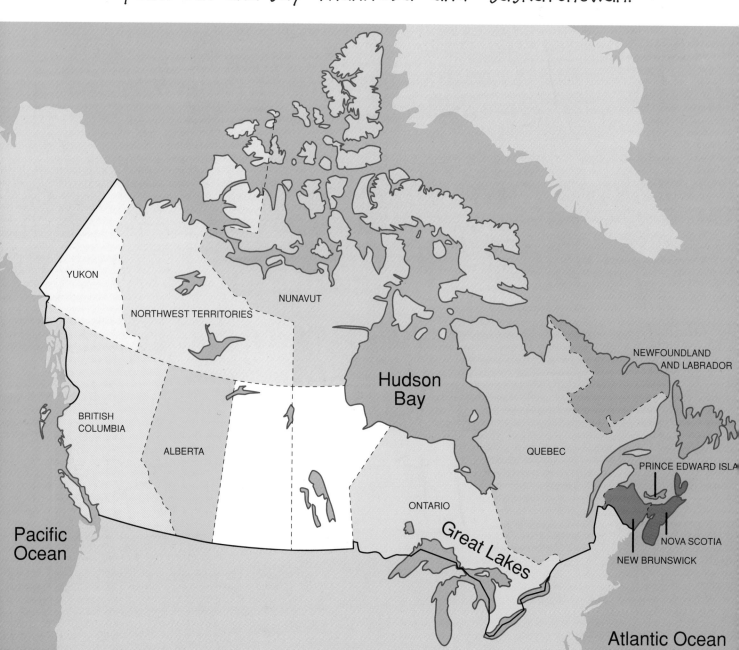

YUKON

NORTHWEST TERRITORIES

NUNAVUT

BRITISH COLUMBIA

ALBERTA

Hudson Bay

NEWFOUNDLAND AND LABRADOR

QUEBEC

PRINCE EDWARD ISLA

ONTARIO

Great Lakes

NOVA SCOTIA

NEW BRUNSWICK

Pacific Ocean

Atlantic Ocean

Banff National Park, Calgary, and Vancouver

Facts Banff National Park is the first national park in Canada. Calgary is the biggest city in Alberta Province. Vancouver is a seaport city and the biggest city in British Columbia Province.

 Paste the stickers to complete the map. After pasting, point out and say "Banff National Park," "Calgary," and "Vancouver."

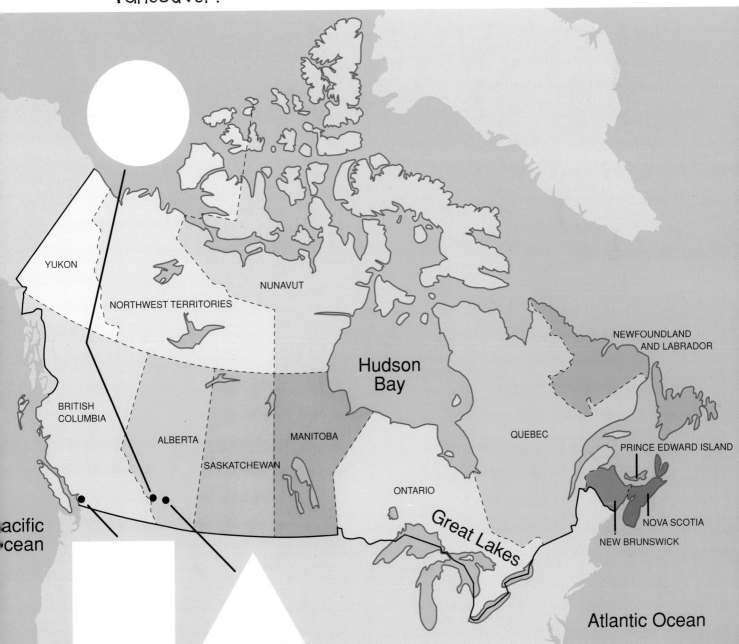

YUKON

NORTHWEST TERRITORIES

NUNAVUT

BRITISH COLUMBIA

ALBERTA

SASKATCHEWAN

MANITOBA

Hudson Bay

ONTARIO

QUEBEC

NEWFOUNDLAND AND LABRADOR

PRINCE EDWARD ISLAND

NOVA SCOTIA

NEW BRUNSWICK

Great Lakes

Pacific Ocean

Atlantic Ocean

British Columbia Parliament Buildings

Facts The British Columbia Parliament Buildings are located in Victoria. Many tourists visit the Parliament Buildings each year.

Draw a line through the maze from the arrow (➡) to the star (★). After finishing, say "British Columbia Parliament Buildings."

United States of America

Facts This page shows all states, cities, landmarks, and landforms in this book. Note that Alaska is scaled down in the map below.

Paste a sticker onto your four favorite places. Tell a parent or friend about them.

Canada

Facts This page shows all provinces, territories, cities, landmarks, and landforms in this book.

Paste a sticker onto your two favorite places. Tell a parent or friend about them.

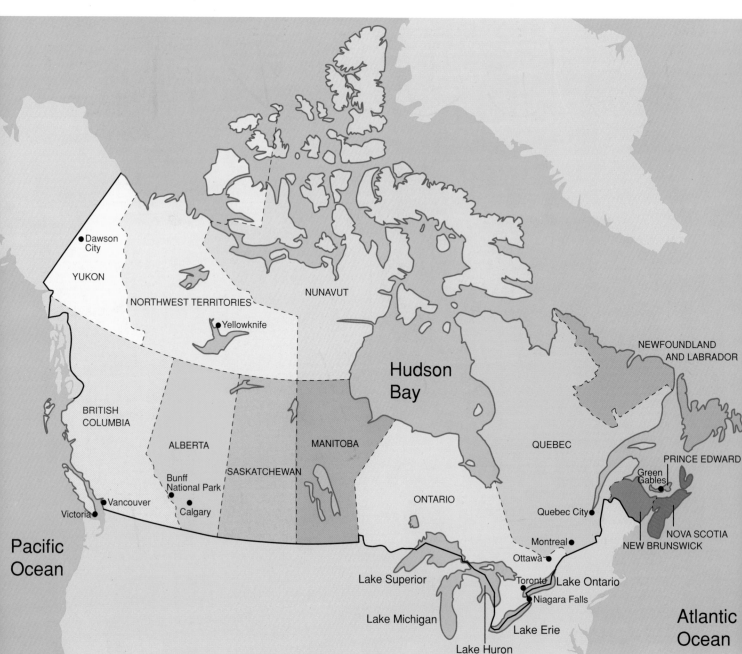

Dawson City

YUKON

NORTHWEST TERRITORIES

NUNAVUT

Yellowknife

NEWFOUNDLAND AND LABRADOR

Hudson Bay

BRITISH COLUMBIA

ALBERTA

SASKATCHEWAN

MANITOBA

QUEBEC

PRINCE EDWARD

Bunff National Park

Green Gables

Vancouver

Calgary

Victoria

ONTARIO

Quebec City

NOVA SCOTIA

NEW BRUNSWICK

Pacific Ocean

Montreal

Ottawa

Lake Superior

Toronto Lake Ontario

Niagara Falls

Lake Michigan

Lake Erie

Atlantic Ocean

Lake Huron

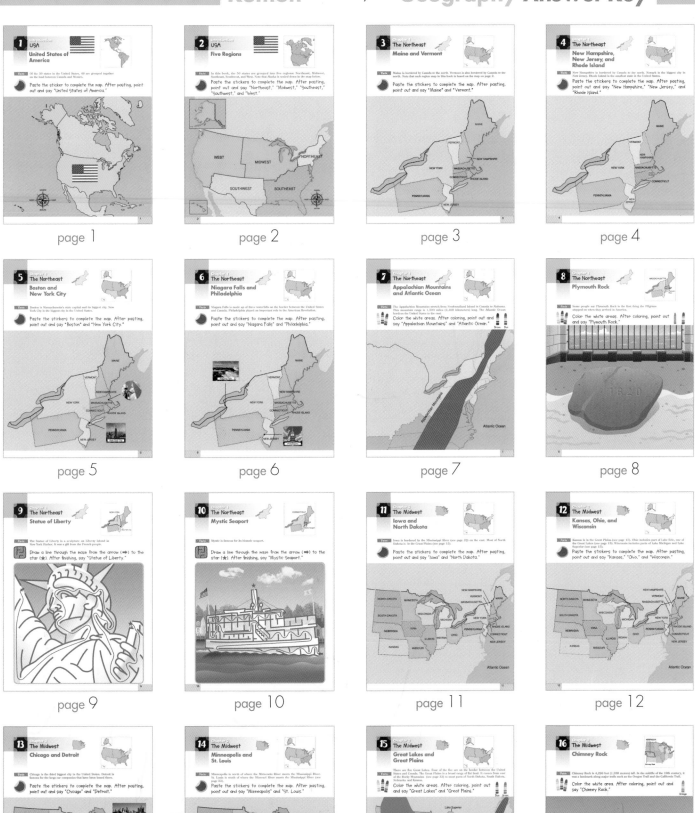

page 1

page 2

page 3

page 4

page 5

page 6

page 7

page 8

page 9

page 10

page 11

page 12

page 13

page 14

page 15

page 16

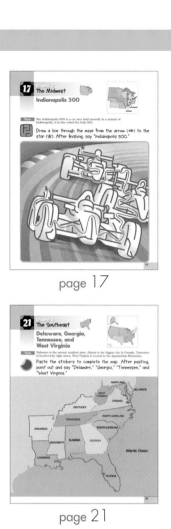

page 17

page 18

page 19

page 20

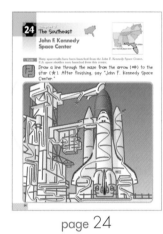

page 21

page 22

page 23

page 24

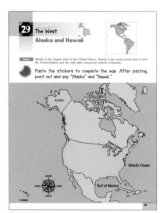

page 25

page 26

page 27

page 28

page 29

page 30

page 31

page 32

page 33

page 34

page 35

page 36

page 37

page 38

page 39

page 40

page 41

page 42

page 43

page 44

page 45

page 46

page 47

page 48

51

Certificate
of
Achievement

TWeedle

is hereby congratulated on completing

Kumon Sticker Activity Books

GEOGRAPHY
U. S. and Canada

Presented on _____ , 20 _____

_____
Parent or Guardian

TWeedledum

Gent
lemonFish
Frog
Deverh M
on
Boyard

To be used in **1**

To be used in **2**

WEST

MIDWEST

SOUTHEAST

To be used in **3**

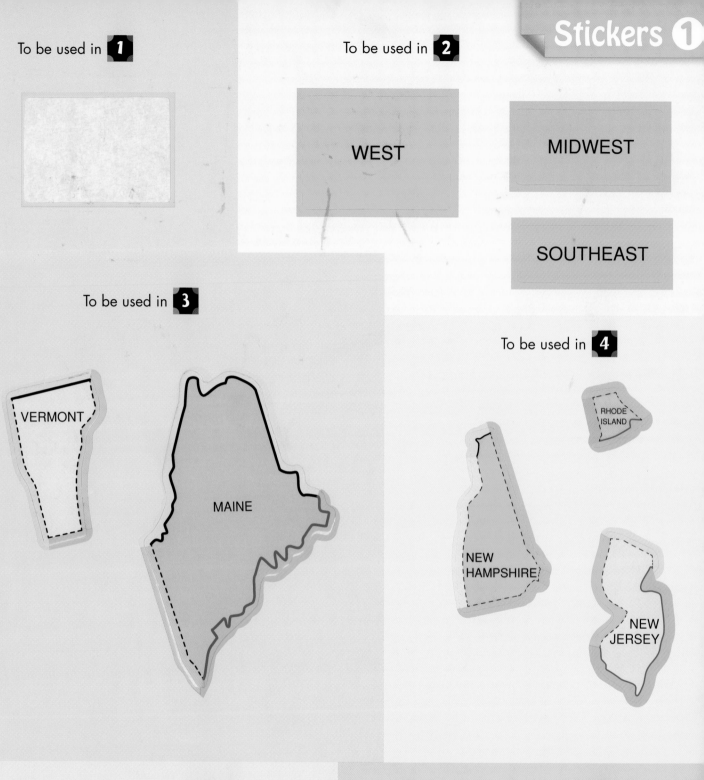

VERMONT

MAINE

To be used in **4**

RHODE ISLAND

NEW HAMPSHIRE

NEW JERSEY

To be used in **5**

Boston

New York City

To be used in **6**

Niagara Falls

Philadelphia

ve geta
ble Exec
ution er

To be used in **11**

NORTH DAKOTA

IOWA

To be used in **12**

KANSAS

OHIO

WISCONSIN

To be used in **13**

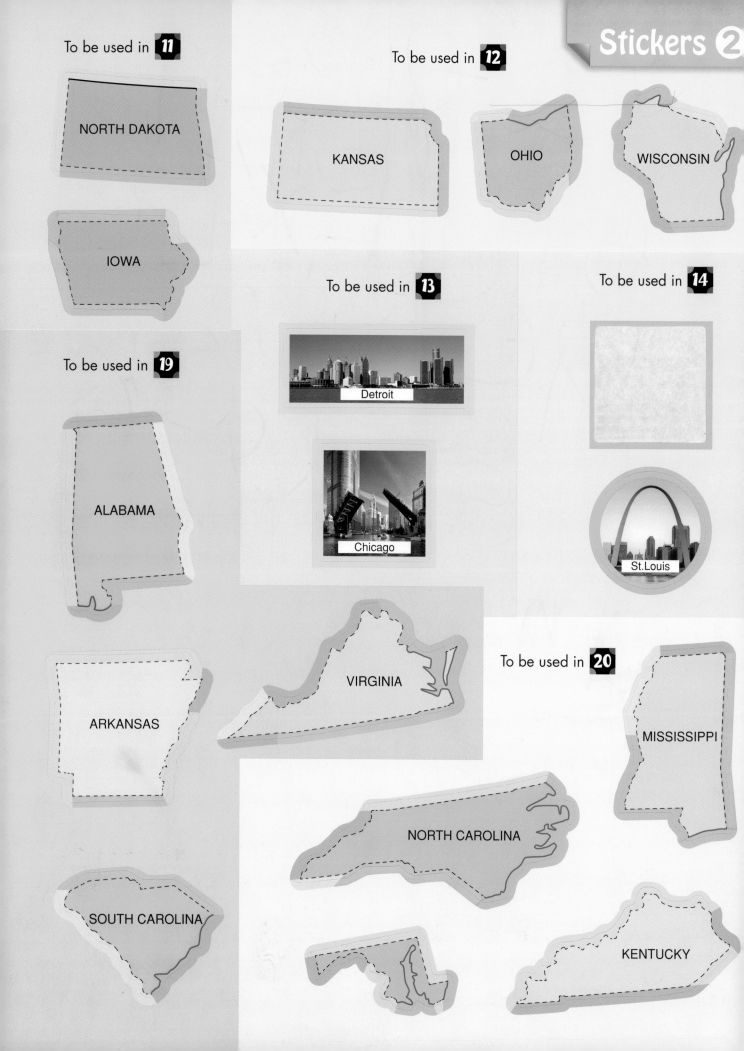

Detroit

Chicago

To be used in **14**

St.Louis

To be used in **19**

ALABAMA

ARKANSAS

VIRGINIA

To be used in **20**

MISSISSIPPI

NORTH CAROLINA

SOUTH CAROLINA

KENTUCKY

To be used in **21**

WEST VIRGINIA

GEORGIA

To be used in **22**

Washington, D.C.

New Orleans

To be used in **26**

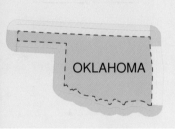

OKLAHOMA

NEW MEXICO

To be used in **27**

Dallas

Houston

To be used in **29**

To be used in **30**

COLORADO

OREGON

To be used in **31**

San Francisco

Los Angeles

To be used in **32**

Honolulu

Knight

Chess piece